D0116228

RARY

FUN & CREATIVE
WORKSHOP ACTIVITIES

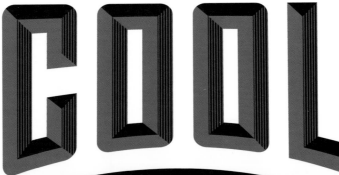

COOL
BATTERY & ELECTRICITY
PROJECTS

REBECCA FELIX

Checkerboard
Library

An Imprint of Abdo Publishing
abdopublishing.com

ABDOPUBLISHING.COM

Published by Abdo Publishing, a division of ABDO, PO Box 398166, Minneapolis, Minnesota 55439. Copyright © 2017 by Abdo Consulting Group, Inc. International copyrights reserved in all countries. No part of this book may be reproduced in any form without written permission from the publisher. Checkerboard Library™ is a trademark and logo of Abdo Publishing.

Printed in the United States of America, North Mankato, Minnesota
062016
092016

 THIS BOOK CONTAINS RECYCLED MATERIALS

Design and Production: Mighty Media, Inc.
Series Editor: Paige V. Polinsky
Photo Credits: Rebecca Felix, Paige V. Polinsky, Shutterstock

The following manufacturers/names appearing in this book are trademarks: DeWALT®, Duracell®, Duro®, Energizer®, Sharpie®

Library of Congress Cataloging-in-Publication Data

Names: Felix, Rebecca, 1984-
Title: Cool battery & electricity projects : fun & creative workshop activities / Rebecca Felix.
Other titles: Cool battery and electricity projects
Description: Minneapolis, Minnesota : Abdo Publishing, [2017] | Series: Cool industrial arts | Includes index.
Identifiers: LCCN 2016006195 (print) | LCCN 2016015738 (ebook) | ISBN 9781680781250 (print) | ISBN 9781680775457 (ebook)
Subjects: LCSH: Electricity--Experiments--Juvenile literature. | Electronics--Experiments--Juvenile literature. | Science projects--Juvenile literature.
Classification: LCC QC527.2 .F448 2017 (print) | LCC QC527.2 (ebook) | DDC
  621.3078--dc23
LC record available at https://lccn.loc.gov/2016006195

TO ADULT HELPERS

This is your chance to help children learn about industrial arts! They will also develop new skills, gain confidence, and make cool things. These activities are designed to teach children how to work with batteries. Readers may need more assistance for some activities than others. Be there to offer guidance when they need it. Encourage them to do as much as they can on their own. Be a cheerleader for their creativity!

Look at the beginning of each project for its difficulty rating (EASY, INTERMEDIATE, ADVANCED).

TABLE (OF) CONTENTS

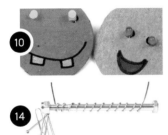

BATTERIES + ELECTRICITY

People made discoveries about and experimented with electricity thousands of years ago. Today, we use electricity every day. Look around you! How many things do you see plugged in? How many **gadgets** run on batteries? Cell phones, watches, refrigerators, toasters, lights, and hundreds of other things are powered by electricity.

WORKING WITH ELECTRICITY

Workshop Tips

It is important to set up a safe workspace before beginning any project **involving** electricity. Find a flat space with plenty of room to work. It could be in the garage, at the kitchen table, or in the basement. Just make sure you get **permission**! Then, follow the tips below to work safely.

- Read materials lists and directions carefully! You don't want to use items with too high a **voltage**.

- If you do get shocked, make sure to tell an adult, especially if it causes a burn on your skin or a tingling feeling.

- Make sure your hands are dry when working with wires and batteries. Keep all liquids away from your workspace too. Liquids can create shocks or cause electric items to burn out.

- Check all batteries and bulbs you use for damage. Check wires for worn or ragged areas.

- Most importantly, *always be alert!* Pay attention to the materials you have in hand, and keep **stripped** wires from touching each other.

Essential Safety Gear

- Gloves

- Safety goggles

- Face mask

- Closed-toe shoes

Be Prepared

- Read the entire project before you begin.

- Make sure you have everything you need to do the project.

- Follow the directions carefully.

- Clean up after you are finished.

ADULT HELPERS

Working with electricity can be **dangerous**. Electricity can produce sparks, shock you, or even start fires. That means you should have an adult standing by for some of these projects.

KEY SYMBOLS

In this book, you may see one or more symbols at the beginning of a project. Here is what they mean:

HOT
This project requires hot tools. Handle with caution.

SAFETY GOGGLES
Eye protection should be worn for certain steps in this project.

TOOLS OF THE TRADE

Here are some of the materials you will need for the projects in this book.

3.5-VOLT WATCH BATTERY

4-WATT WEDGE BASE LIGHT BULB

9-VOLT BATTERY

BARE (OR STRIPPED) COPPER WIRE

BUZZER

D BATTERIES

ELECTRICAL TAPE

HAMMER

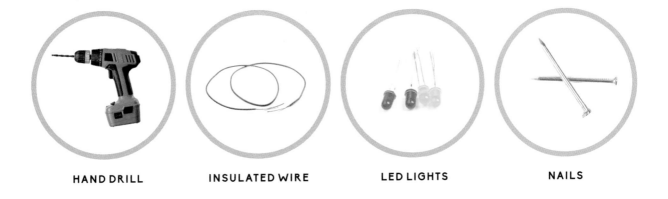

HAND DRILL　　　**INSULATED WIRE**　　　**LED LIGHTS**　　　**NAILS**

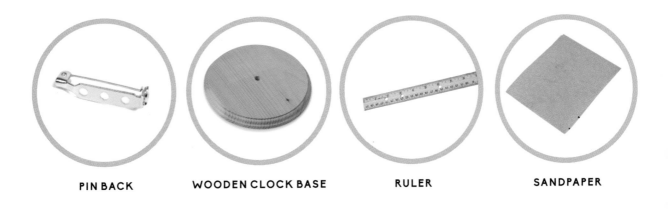

PIN BACK　　　**WOODEN CLOCK BASE**　　　**RULER**　　　**SANDPAPER**

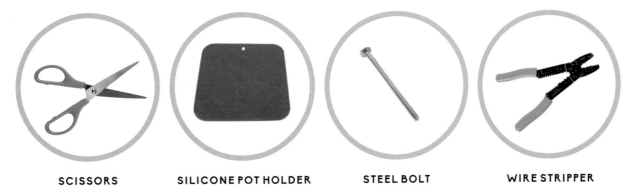

SCISSORS　　　**SILICONE POT HOLDER**　　　**STEEL BOLT**　　　**WIRE STRIPPER**

LED
EMOTI-PIN

CONNECT BRIGHT
LED LIGHTS TO A
BATTERY AND MAKE
A BUTTON EMOTICON
WITH LIGHT-UP EYES!

MATERIALS

- pencil
- round lid or container
- cardboard
- ruler
- scissors
- markers
- hole punch

- 2 10mm LED lights, any color
- 3.5-volt watch battery
- electrical tape
- pin back

MAKING THE FACE

1 Trace a round lid or container of any size onto the cardboard. Or, use a ruler to draw a square or rectangle. Cut out the shape.

2 Draw a face on your shape. Make two dots where you'd like the eyes to be. Then use the hole punch to make holes over the marks.

3 Color the pin with markers.

Continued on the next page.

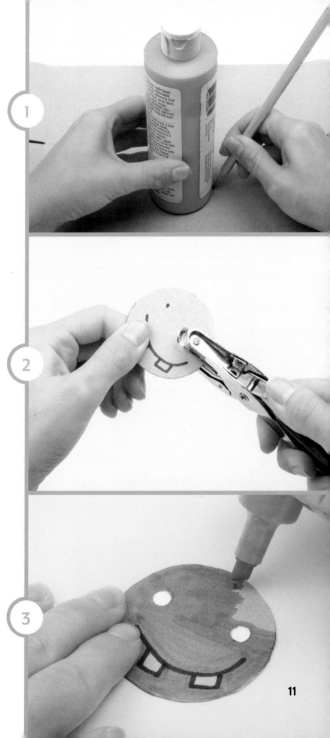

11

CONNECTING THE LIGHTS + BATTERY

1 Test the LED lights and battery. Place each LED's longer wire on the positive side of the battery, which has a "+" sign. Then touch the short wire to the opposite, or negative, side. If the LEDs do not light up, you may need to use a different light or battery!

2 Tape the pin back to the positive side of the battery.

3 Push one LED through each eye hole. Bend the long wires so they stick out to the sides. Cross the short wires, and press them against the cardboard.

4 Tape the battery to the cardboard over the crossed wires.

5 Carefully bend the long LED wires. Tuck one wire into each of the small holes at the ends of the pin. This connects the LED to the battery using the pin as a **conductor**.

6 Attach your LED pin to your shirt, jacket, or backpack. To save the battery, unhook the long wires tucked into the pin. Hook the wires again to make the LEDs light up!

TIP
Check electronic stores for LEDs that flash in multiple colors!

MAGIC MAGNET

CREATE A COOL
MAGNET FROM A MIX
OF METALS, WIRE,
AND A BATTERY!

MATERIALS

- scissors
- silicone pot holder
- ruler
- marker
- 100-grit sandpaper
- bare or stripped copper wire
- large steel bolt

- nut to fit the bolt
- D battery
- electrical tape
- rubber bands
- several small metal items to pick up with the magnet: paper clips, small nails, bobby pins

PREPPING

1 Cut the silicone pot holder into a rectangle. Make it 4 by 5½ inches (10.2 by 14 cm).

2 Screw the nut onto the bolt.

WRAPPING + BENDING THE WIRE

1 Wrap the middle of the wire around the bolt several times. Make sure there is at least 6 inches (15 cm) of wire remaining on each end.

Continued on the next page.

15

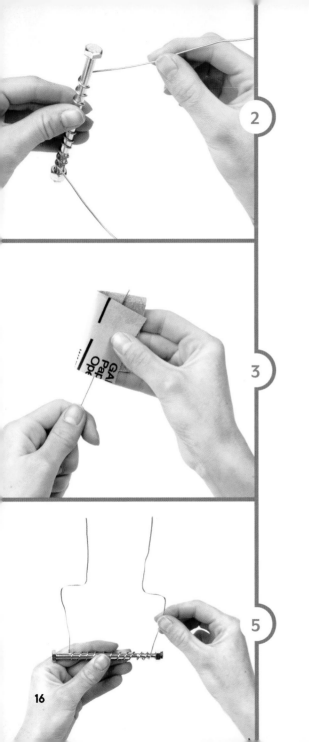

2 Make sure both ends of the wire point in the same direction. If one end is much longer than the other, trim it so both are about the same length.

3 Sand 4 inches (10.2 cm) of each end of the wire.

4 One inch (2.5 cm) from where you stopped sanding, bend one wire end toward the other. Repeat with the other end of the wire.

5 About ½ inch (1.3 cm) from each bend, turn each end of the wire up again.

CONNECTING + WRAPPING

1 Wrap one end of the wire around the battery's positive **terminal**. Make sure the wire is looped and touching the terminal knob.

2 Tape the wire down very tightly. Make sure the wire will not move off the terminal.

3 Cut a piece of tape about 8 inches (20.3 cm) long. Place the tape's middle to the positive terminal. Stretch the tape ends down the length of the battery. Leave the ends hanging loose above the negative battery end. This tape will hold down a piece of wire later.

4 Wrap the silicone rectangle around the battery. Secure it with rubber bands.

Continued on the next page.

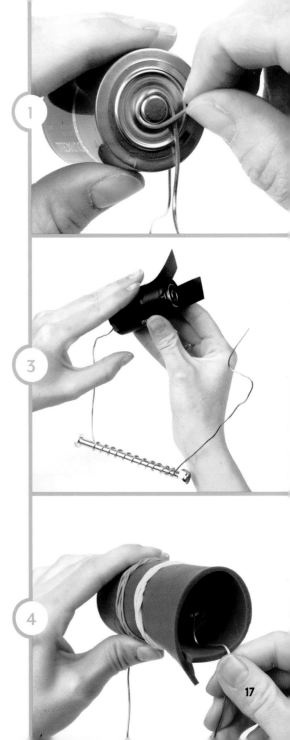

COMPLETING + USING

1 Place the loose end of the wire on the negative end of the battery. Make sure the wire is touching the negative **terminal**.

2 Tape the wire to the battery very tightly. Work quickly! The battery and wire will begin to get hot.

3 The bolt should now be magnetic! Test it by picking up the small metal items you gathered. Hold the magnet ONLY by the silicone handle. The bolt, wire, and battery will get very hot!

4 This **gadget** gets hot when its **circuit** is connected. It's safest to leave it unconnected when not in use. Have an adult help you pull the wire off of the negative end of the battery. When you're ready to use the magnet again, just re-tape the wire onto the negative terminal!

19

TIP

If the bolt does not work, check the wire connections. You can also try taking it apart and sanding the wire ends a bit more.

BUZZING
TWEEZERS + TRAY
GAME

REMOVE COINS AND TRINKETS FROM A WIRE-WRAPPED ICE CUBE TRAY. DON'T BUMP THE WIRE, OR YOU'LL SET OFF THE BUZZER!

MATERIALS

- 100-grit sandpaper
- 12' to 15' (3.7 to 4.6 m) bare or stripped 22-gauge copper wire
- ruler
- electrical tape
- ice cube tray
- wire stripper
- 3VDC mini buzzer
- D battery
- 2' (0.6 m) insulated copper wire (speaker wire works well)
- metal tweezers
- several small metal trinkets

INTERMEDIATE

WRAPPING THE TRAY

1 Sand one end of the bare copper wire.

2 Measure 5 inches (12.7 cm) from the sanded end of the wire. Tape that spot to one corner of the ice cube tray. Starting at that point, begin to wrap the wire around the tray in a crisscross pattern. Wrap until all the wire is used up. Twist the loose end around another part of the wire.

ATTACHING THE BUZZER + BATTERY

1 **Strip** the end of each buzzer wire.

Continued on the next page.

21

2 Connect one buzzer wire to the copper wire end, making sure the **stripped** parts of both wires are touching. Seal the wires together with electrical tape.

3 Tape the other buzzer wire to the positive **terminal** on the battery. Make sure the stripped part is touching the terminal knob.

ATTACHING THE TWEEZERS

1 Use the wire stripper to strip 1 inch (2.5 cm) from each end of the **insulated** wire.

2 Wrap one stripped end around the end of the tweezers. Tape it securely in place.

3 Attach the other **stripped** end of the **insulated** wire to the negative **terminal** on the battery. Make sure to tape it securely.

PLAYING THE GAME

1 Put a metal trinket in each cup of ice cube tray.

2 Use the tweezers to remove the trinkets without setting off the buzzer. For a greater challenge, add larger metal objects to remove!

TIP

Buzzer not working? Make sure the end of the copper wire attached to the buzzer is sanded enough. You can also sand the end of the tweezers where the wire is attached.

3

2

MOUNTED
MASON JAR LIGHT

BUILD AND WIRE YOUR
OWN LAMP WITH A
WORKING SWITCH!

MATERIALS

- acrylic paint
- paintbrush
- wooden clock base, about 7" (17.8 cm) across
- mason jar with lid
- scrap wood or cutting board
- wood clamp
- marker
- hand drill
- wood glue
- large paper clip
- hammer
- 2 brass nails
- 1" to 2" (2.5 to 5 cm) hook-and-loop tape
- ruler
- 24" (61 cm) 22-gauge insulated copper bell wire
- scissors
- wire stripper
- 9-**volt** battery
- electrical tape
- 4-watt wedge base bulb
- duct tape
- 4 adhesive foam squares

PREPARING
THE BASE + LID

I Paint the wood clock fun colors. Let it dry. This will be your lamp's base.

2 Remove the separate band from the jar lid. Clamp the disk part to the scrap wood or cutting board. Mark and drill a hole through the center of the lid.

3 Unclamp the disk and reassemble the lid. Glue the lid onto the wood base upside down, so the open side faces up. Keep the center holes of the lid and wood base lined up.

Continued on the next page.

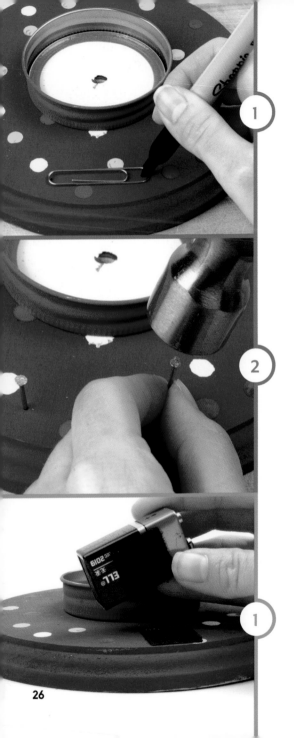

BUILDING THE SWITCH

1 Place the paper clip on top of the wood base with its long side facing the base's edge. Use the marker to make two small dots inside the paper clip, one at each end. Make sure the dots touch the ends of the paper clip.

2 Remove the paper clip. Hammer a brass nail into each dot. Stop when the nails are pounded about halfway in.

WIRE WORK

Use the hook-and-loop tape to attach the battery to the wood base. Place it about 4 inches (10.2 cm) from one of the brass nails.

2 Separate red and white strands of the copper bell wire. Cut two 10-inch (25.4 cm) pieces of red wire and one 4.5 inch (11.5 cm) piece of white wire. **Strip** both ends of all three pieces.

3 Connect the end of one piece of red wire to the positive battery **terminal**. Secure with electrical tape.

4 Run the other end of the wire over the edge of the base and up through the base's hole. Leave the wire sticking up out of the center hole.

Continued on the next page.

27

5 Connect the end of the white piece of wire to the negative **terminal** on the battery. Secure with electrical tape.

6 Wrap the other end of the white wire around the closest nail.

7 Wrap one end of the second red wire around the other nail. Then run the other end of that red wire over the edge of the wood base. Thread it up through the center hole, along with the first red wire.

CONNECTING THE BULB + FINISHING

1 Bend one of the bulb's metal prongs around one red wire end. Bend the other prong around the other red wire's end.

2 Place the paper clip on the base so it hooks around both nails. The bulb should light up! If it does not, check all the connections.

3 Unhook the paper clip. Turn the wood base upside down. Tape the wires down with duct tape. Then stick the four foam squares on the bottom of the base. Space them evenly around the edge. This will keep the lamp from wobbling.

Continued on the next page.

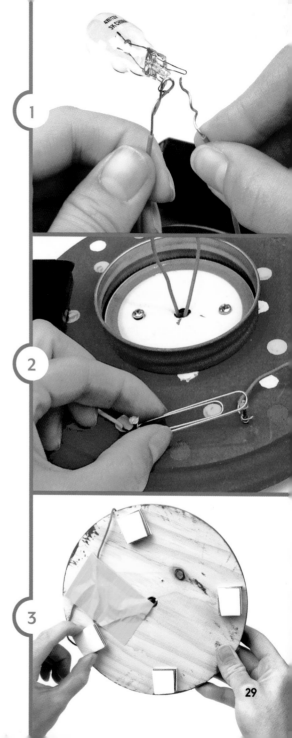

4 Screw the jar onto the lid. Then move your paper clip switch to "on"! Turn out the lights and **admire** your work!

5 Don't forget to turn your paper clip switch "off" to save the battery. If the battery dies, replace it with a new one. If the bulb burns out, unscrew the jar and connect a new bulb.

OPTIONAL
You can decorate your lamp with paint, glitter, or stickers! Or, you can leave your lamp unpainted to see the bulb and wiring. This will give your light an industrial look!

GLOSSARY

ADMIRE – to like or be pleased with something.

CIRCUIT – a system made of parts that, when connected, allow an electrical current to flow.

CONDUCTOR – a substance or object that electricity, heat, or sound can pass through.

DANGEROUS – able or likely to cause harm or injury.

GADGET – a small tool that does a particular job.

INSULATED – to be covered with a material in order to stop heat, electricity, or sound from going in or out.

INVOLVE – to have or include as a part of something.

PERMISSION – when a person in charge says it's okay to do something.

STRIP – to remove a wire's insulating outer layer. A stripped wire has had its outer layer removed.

TERMINAL – a device attached to the end of things for the purpose of making an electrical connection.

VOLTAGE – the force of an electrical current, expressed in volts.

Websites

To learn more about Cool Industrial Arts, visit **booklinks.abdopublishing.com**. These links are routinely monitored and updated to provide the most current information available.

INDEX